TALES FROM PEOPLE AND PLACES

HELLO ENGLISH SCHOOL

di Anna Pia Carfagnini e Walter Padula

Hello English School
di Anna Pia Carfagnini
e Walter Padula
86039 - Termoli (CB)
www.helloenglishlanguage.com

"Tales from people and places "
Autori: Walter Padula e Anna Pia Carfagnini
Anno di Pubblicazione: 2023

COME SCARICARE LE TRACCE AUDIO

Vai sul sito www.helloenglishlanguage.com / DOWNLOAD / AUDIOBOOK
oppure scansiona il codice QR

INTRODUZIONE

Immagina di viaggiare nel tempo e nello spazio, esplorando storie che hanno plasmato il mondo in cui viviamo, e di farlo con la lingua che unisce il pianeta: l'inglese. Ora, questa opportunità è a portata di mano, imparando l'inglese attraverso racconti e narrazioni.

Con il nostro metodo, ogni lezione diventa un'avventura. Leggerai affascinanti storie di persone, luoghi e civiltà che hanno radicalmente cambiato il nostro modo di vivere. Conoscerai le motivazioni di inventori e scopritori, esplorerai antiche civiltà e imparerai da eroi di tutti i giorni che hanno spostato montagne con la loro tenacia. E tutto ciò mentre impari l'inglese, una lingua che si è evoluta parallelamente a questi incredibili eventi.

Ma non si tratta solo di lettura. Ogni storia è un pezzo di un percorso educativo progettato per permetterti di comprendere, assorbire e praticare la lingua inglese. Dopo ogni lettura, troverai esercizi di comprensione che costruiranno la tua sicurezza con l'inglese reale, parlato da milioni di persone in tutto il mondo.

Inoltre, ogni lezione è un'opportunità per familiarizzare con un elemento fondamentale ma spesso enigmatico della lingua inglese: i *phrasal verbs*. Questi verbi sono essenziali per chiunque voglia padroneggiare l'inglese e ogni storia ne introdurrà uno nuovo, contestualizzandolo in modo che la sua comprensione e memorizzazione siano naturali e intuitive.

Attraverso questo viaggio, l'inglese sarà un'avventura che aspetta solo di essere vissuta. E tutto ciò che serve per iniziare è il desiderio di aprire un libro e lasciarsi trasportare dalle parole.

INDICE

THE AMAZON RAINFOREST

"THE LUNG
OF THE EARTH"

THE AMAZON RAINFOREST

The Amazon Forest is a very big and special place in South America. It is like a giant home for many animals and plants. The trees are very tall, and the Amazon River flows through it. People say it's the "lung of the Earth" because it makes a lot of oxygen. This is important for people and animals to breathe.

Many unique and different trees and animals live there. People have lived in the Amazon for a very long time. They know a lot about the forest and how to use the plants for medicine and food.

But, there are problems in the Amazon. Some people cut down the trees. They do this to get wood and make space for farms. This is not good because it hurts the animals and makes the air not clean.

The Amazon is also having many fires. Some are natural, but some are because people want more space for things like farms. This is very bad for the animals and the air. Many people and groups want to help the Amazon. They want to stop cutting down trees and make rules to protect the animals.

The people who live in the Amazon are very important. They have their homes there, and they know how to live with the forest. Their ways are special and help keep the Amazon healthy. It's important to listen to the people who live there and work together to protect the Amazon.

People from all around the world are learning about the Amazon and trying to help. They want to stop the cutting of trees and make sure the animals have a safe place to live. Governments are also making rules to protect the forest. It's a big challenge because the Amazon is so big, but it's an important job. The Amazon Forest is like a treasure for the whole world, and we need to take care of it together.

WHAT DID YOU LEARN?

Are these sentences **T**rue or **F**alse?

The Amazon Forest is in North America.
It is home to many animals and plants.
The Amazon River is a lake in Canada.
The forest is called the "lungs of the Earth".
People have never lived in the Forest.
Some people cut down trees.
All fires in the Amazon are natural.
There are groups that want to protect the wildlife.
There are a few species of animals.
Governments are trying to protect the Forest.

PHRASAL VERB OF THE DAY

Look after: to take care of someone or something, to make sure they are safe and healthy.

We need to look after the Amazon Forest because it is home to many plants and animals.

YOUR NOTES:

_____

_____

_____

LIFE ON A
SPACE STATION

"LIFE OVER

THE EARTH"

LIFE ON A SPACE STATION

The space station is where astronauts from different countries live and work together in the space.

Living in microgravity

One of the biggest differences about life on a space station is the concept of microgravity. On Earth, gravity keeps us grounded, but in space, there is a sensation of floating. On a space station they have microgravity: imagine them eating, sleeping, and even exercising while floating in the air!

The International Space Station (ISS)

The International Space Station, or ISS, is a symbol of international cooperation. It's a large spacecraft that orbits Earth, and it is the home and workplace for astronauts. The ISS is a project which involves space agencies from the United States, Russia, Europe, Japan, and Canada. Astronauts live together in the space and they conduct scientific experiments and learn about life in space.

Daily routines

Life on a space station follows a schedule to ensure that everything runs fine. Astronauts start their day with personal hygiene activities like brushing teeth and washing. Water doesn't flow in the same way as it does on Earth, so astronauts use no-rinse shampoo and wipes for bathing.

After personal care, astronauts start their works. They conduct experiments, maintain the spacecraft, and communicate with Earth. They have also to do physical exercise to keep their muscles and bones healthy.

Challenges in space

Living on a space station has a lot of challenges. Microgravity affects the human body in various ways, such as fluid shifts, changes in vision, and weakening of muscles. Astronauts must adapt to these conditions.

Another challenge is the feeling of lonely. Astronauts spend months on the space station, away from their families and friends. The communication is through video calls and email. Maintaining mental health is a priority, and astronauts participate in activities like watching movies, reading, and enjoying Earth's breathtaking views from space.

Scientific discoveries

One of the primary purposes of a space station is to conduct scientific experiments in microgravity. Scientists use this unique environment to learn about phenomena that are impossible to study on Earth. The ISS contributes significantly to our knowledge of the science and universe.

Returning to Earth

Astronauts usually spend several months on the space station before returning to Earth. The return journey involves re-entering the Earth's atmosphere, which can be a turbulent experience. The advanced technology ensures them a safe return.

In conclusion, life on a space station is an extraordinary adventure that challenges the limits of human capability. As technology advances, our understanding of space and our ability to live, continues to grow.

WHAT DID YOU LEARN?

Are these sentences **T**rue or **F**alse?

Astronauts experience the sensation of floating.
The ISS stands for "Intergalactic Space Shuttle."
Only astronauts from the U.S. live on the ISS.
Astronauts face the feeling of loneliness.
Water flows in the same way as it does on Earth.
Astronauts use regular shampoo.
The main purpose of the ISS is to take a vacation.
On the ISS, astronauts conduct experiments.
Microgravity can cause changes in the vision.
Astronauts spend years on the space station.

PHRASAL VERB OF THE DAY

Float around: to move or fly slowly in the air without a clear direction, like a balloon in the sky.

In the ISS, astronauts float around due to the effects of microgravity.

YOUR NOTES:

_____

_____

_____

MAHATMA GANDHI

"THE GREAT SOUL"

CHAPTER 3

MAHATMA GANDHI

Long time ago in India, there was a man named Mahatma Gandhi. He was born on October 2nd, 1869, in a small town called Porbandar. Gandhi was a wise and kind person who wanted to help people and make the world a better place.

When Gandhi was a boy, he liked to play and learn new things. His family was not rich, but they were happy. They taught him important values like honesty and hard work.

As Gandhi grew up, he went to school and then travelled to London to study law. In London, he learned many things and met people from different countries. This made him think that everyone should be treated equally, no matter where they came from.

Later Gandhi went to South Africa to work as a lawyer. There he saw that some people were treated badly because of their skin colour so he decided to do something about it. Gandhi started to speak up for the rights of all people.
Gandhi believed in a powerful idea: non-violence. This means solving problems without hurting anyone.

He encouraged people to stand up for what is right but to do it peacefully. Gandhi wore simple clothes and lived a simple life to show that you don't need fancy things to be a good person.

One of the most famous things Gandhi did was the Salt March in 1930, in Britain. Gandhi and some other people, made their own salt. It was against the British rules. In fact, at that time, only the British government could sell salt.

Gandhi's ideas inspired many people, and he became known as "Mahatma," which means "great soul." He wanted India to be free from British rule, but he didn't want to fight with violence. Instead, he led peaceful protests and asked people to be brave and kind.

In 1947, India gained its independence, and Gandhi was very happy. He also wanted people of different religions to live together in peace. Sadly, in 1948, a person who disagreed with Gandhi's ideas took his life.
Today, the 2nd of October, is a special day in India, and people around the world remember him as a great leader who believed in peace, kindness, and equality for all.

WHAT DID YOU LEARN?
Are these sentences **T**rue or **F**alse?

Mahatma Gandhi was born in a big city in India.
Gandhi's family taught him to be dishonest.
Gandhi studied medicine in London.
He spent a part of his life in South Africa.
Gandhi believed in using violence.
Gandhi wore fancy clothes and live a luxurious life.
"Salt March" was held in 1930 in India.
Only the government could sell salt in Britain.
Gandhi wanted India to remain under British rule.
Gandhi died because of a mad man.

PHRASAL VERB OF THE DAY

Stand up for: to defend or support a particular cause or person.

Gandhi stood up for the rights of all people, especially those who were treated unfairly due to their skin colour.

YOUR NOTES:

_____

_____

_____

THE WHITE HOUSE

"ICONIC, PRESIDENTIAL, HISTORIC"

CHAPTER 4

THE WHITE HOUSE

The White House is a special building in the United States, in Washington, D.C.. It is the home of the President of the United States. It is big and white. People around the world know the White House as a symbol of the United States.

The beginning

In the past the United States did not have a president's house, so people decided to build a house for the president George Washington. They started building the White House in 1792.

Many people helped build the White House and worked very hard. It took eight years to build it. The second president, John Adams, was the first president to live there in 1800.

A difficult time

In 1814, there was a war with the United Kingdom. British soldiers came to Washington, D.C. and set fire to the White House, which damaged it. After the war, people had to fix the White House.

Changes and presidents

Many years passed. Many presidents lived in the White House. Each president and his family brought something new. They changed furniture, they added paintings, they made the White House beautiful, taking care of it.

The president Theodore Roosevelt made big changes. He wanted more space so he built new rooms. He also gave the White House its name in 1901. Before that, people called it the "President's Palace" or "President's House."

The White House today

Today, the White House is more than a house. It has 132 rooms. There is a big office for the president, called the Oval Office. There are rooms for meetings and also places for the president's people to work.

The Oval Office

The Oval Office is one of the most famous and important parts of the White House. It is the official residence and workplace of the President of the United States, where he conducts daily business, meets with staff, political leaders, guests and other visiting officials. Here, the most crucial decisions affecting the country and sometimes the world, are made.

Tourists from all over the world come to see it. However, they can go inside only in special occasions. The White House is not just the President's building. It is an important piece of history.

WHAT DID YOU LEARN?

Are these sentences **T**rue or **F**alse?

The White House is in New York City.
It was originally built for President John Adams.
It took two years to build.
British soldiers painted the White House in 1814.
All presidents changed paintings and furniture.
It was always called "The White House".
The White House has 50 rooms.
The Oval Office is where the president sleeps.
Tourists can go inside to visit every day.
The White House has no historical significance.

PHRASAL VERB OF THE DAY

Set up: establishing or creating something.

People set up the White House as the official residence for the President of the United States in 1792.

YOUR NOTES:

_____

_____

_____

HINDUISM

"PEACE AND

RESPECT"

HINDUISM

Hinduism is very old and comes from a place called India. Many people in India believe in Hinduism. In fact, it's one of the world's big religions.

Hindus believe in many gods and goddesses. They think these gods are part of one big power which comes in many forms. The three most important gods are Brahma, Vishnu, and Shiva. Brahma is the god who created the world. Vishnu is the god who protects the world. Shiva is the god who can destroy to make new again. Each god has its own job.

Hindus have many holy books, not just one. These books have old stories and songs. They teach people how to live a good life. One famous book is called the 'Bhagavad Gita'. It is a very old book. Many Hindus love it very much.

There is a special symbol in Hinduism. It is called 'Om'. It is very sacred. Hindus say this word when they pray or meditate. Meditation is when people sit quietly and clear their minds. It helps them feel peaceful.

Temples are important places for Hindus. They go there to pray and give offerings. It might be flowers or food. They ring bells and sing songs for the gods. Sometimes, they sit quietly and think about the gods.

Hindus celebrate many festivals. One famous festival is called Diwali. It is a festival of lights. People light small lamps everywhere. They do this to remember that good wins over bad. They eat sweets and give gifts. It is a happy time.

Another big festival is Holi. It is a festival of colours. People throw colourful powder on each other. They laugh, sing, and dance. It is very fun and exciting.

Hindus believe in something called karma. Karma is like a cosmic rule. It says, "What you do comes back to you." If you do good things, good things will happen. If you do bad things, bad things will happen. It teaches people to be good.

Hindus believe in life after death. They think the soul comes back in a new body. This belief is called reincarnation. They believe the soul is born again and again. It learns new lessons each time.

The cow is a special animal in Hinduism. Hindus do not eat beef. They think cows are gentle and give a lot. Cows give milk and help in the fields. So, Hindus respect cows very much.

Hinduism teaches peace and respect for all life. It says every living thing is important. Hindus try to live in peace with everyone. They also respect nature.

Hinduism has many gods, many festivals, and deep beliefs. It teaches love and respect. It is a very interesting religion.

WHAT DID YOU LEARN?

Are these sentences **T**rue or **F**alse?

Hinduism is a new religion from India.
Many gods and goddesses are part of Hinduism.
The 'Bhagavad Gita' is a famous movie in Hinduism.
The special symbol 'Om' is used in singing only.
Hindus go to temples to pray and give offerings.
Diwali is a festival of lights in Hinduism.
During Holi, people throw colourful water.
Karma means that your actions can return to you.
The soul will never comes back after death.
Cows are seen as special and are not eaten.

PHRASAL VERB OF THE DAY

Look up to: to respect or admire someone or something.

Hindus look up to gods like Brahma, Vishnu, and Shiva, respecting their roles in the world.

YOUR NOTES:

_____

_____

_____

WHY BRITISH
LOVE TEA

"TEA FOR EVERYONE"

WHY BRITISH LOVE TEA

Tea is a hot drink made with water and tea leaves. Many people in Britain drink it every day. But have you ever wondered why? Let's find out together!

Over 4,000 years ago, people in China started drinking tea. Much later traders brought tea to Britain. At first, only rich people could buy tea because it was expensive. But later, everyone started drinking it because it became cheaper.

In the 1800s, something called "Afternoon Tea" became popular. This was a time to sit, talk, and drink tea with small foods. It was a happy time for families and friends.

Now, tea is a big part of British life. Many people drink tea when they wake up, at work, or with friends. It helps them feel relaxed. Some also drink tea to feel warm on cold days. In Britain, people drink around 100 million cups of tea every day!

People in Britain love different kinds of tea. The most common one is called "black tea." They often add milk and sometimes sugar. There are also "green tea" and "herbal tea." These are good for the body and have different tastes.

What is Teatime? "Teatime" can mean two things. One is "Afternoon Tea," which happens between lunch and dinner, often around 4 o'clock. People eat small sandwiches, cakes, and cookies with their tea. It is very fancy and fun.

The second "teatime" is also important. For some British people, "teatime" means "dinner time." It is the time when families and children sit down to eat in the evening. They don't always drink tea at this teatime, but they enjoy meals together.

There is also something called a "tea break" at work. It is a short rest from work to drink tea. People chat and relax during the tea break. It makes them happy and ready to work again.

So, why is tea so special in Britain? Tea is more than just a drink there. It is a way to bring families and people together. It is a sign of friendship and care.

It is a warm, nice drink that makes people feel good.

WHAT DID YOU LEARN?

Are these sentences **T**rue or **F**alse?

Tea is made with water and tea leaves.
Tea was first drunk over 4,000 years ago.
In the past, only poor people could buy tea.
"Afternoon Tea" is a time to sit and talk.
British people drink tea only in the morning.
People in Britain do not use "green tea".
"Teatime" is when people drink tea.
During a "tea break", people stop working.
Tea in Britain is a sign of friendship and care.
British drink about 100 cups of tea a day.

PHRASAL VERB OF THE DAY

Wind down: to describe the act of relaxing after a period of activity or stress.

Many people in Britain drink tea to wind down after a long day at work.

YOUR NOTES:

_____

_____

_____

THE FIRST
WORLD WAR

"BATTLES

BEYOND

BORDERS"

THE FIRST WORLD WAR

At the beginning of the 20th century there was a big war called the First World War. It happened from 1914 to 1918. A lot of countries around the world were involved, and it was a very sad time for people.

The war started because some countries did not agree on borders, and they wanted more power. It was not a happy time, and many soldiers had to leave their homes and families to go and fight. They wore uniforms and carried guns.

At the beginning, people thought the war would be quick, but it became much longer and more difficult than anyone expected. Soldiers lived in trenches, which were like long ditches in the ground. It was a hard life, with mud and cold weather making it very hard for the soldiers.

There were two main groups of countries in the war. One was called the Allies, which included countries like France, the United Kingdom, and Russia. The other group was called the Central Powers, which included Germany, Austria-Hungary, and the Ottoman Empire. The war had many battles, and in one of them, soldiers on both sides stopped fighting for a short time during Christmas. It was a moment of peace in the middle of a difficult time.

As the war went on, new weapons and technologies were used, making it even more dangerous. There were airplanes, tanks, and gas masks. These things changed how the war was fought, and it was not easy for the soldiers.

Many people were affected by the war. Families worried about their loved ones, and there was not enough food. People had to ration food, which means they could only have the necessary for the life.

In 1917, a big change happened. The United States joined the war and helped the Allies. With their support, the balance of power started to change. Finally, in 1918, the war came to an end. There was a big celebration, and people were happy that the fighting was over. They hoped it would be the last big war in the world.

The leaders of the countries came together to make peace. They had a meeting in a place called Versailles where they signed a treaty of peace.

People remember the First World War every year with celebration all around the world.

WHAT DID YOU LEARN?
Are these sentences **T**rue or **F**alse?

The First World War started in the 20th century.
The war began to expand the country's borders.
Soldiers did not wear uniforms in the War.
People believed the war would last long time.
The soldiers had a comfortable life in trenches.
The UK and France were part of the Allies.
During one Christmas, the soldiers stopped.
There were no new weapons or technologies.
The United States joined the war in 1917.
The peace treaty was signed in Versailles.

PHRASAL VERB OF THE DAY

Break out: describe situations where something unpleasant or uncontrolled suddenly starts.

The First World War broke out in 1914 due to disagreements among countries.

YOUR NOTES:

_____

_____

_____

THE INDEPENDENCE
DAY

"WE ARE

A BIG FAMILY"

CHAPTER 8

THE INDEPENDENCE DAY

The Independence Day is a public holiday in the United States. It happens every year on July 4th. This day remembers a special moment in history. On July 4th, 1776, America said, "We want to be free!" They did not want to be ruled by British leaders anymore.

Before 1776, America was part of Great Britain. But people wanted to make their own rules so they started the revolution. It was very hard and took many years. In the end, America became a free country. July 4th is the day they declared their independence and they became a new country.

Today the Independence Day is a happy time in the United States. There are many colours: red, white, and blue which are the colours of the American flag.

In the morning, towns have parades. People walk in the streets. They play music, dance, and wave flags.

They wave and cheer. Children and adults like to watch the parades.

For lunch many families get together and have a special meal outside, cooking food on a grill. They eat things like hot dogs and hamburgers. At night there are fireworks that light up all the streets.

On that day, people wear red, white, and blue. These colours show pride in their country. Some people also wear hats or paint their faces.

Families and friends also talk about history. They remember the people who fought for freedom. They think about what it means to be American. It is a day of pride for everyone. They want to be like a big family.

On July 4th, leaders give speeches. They talk about the past and remember the people who fought for freedom. They also think about the future and say: "Let's make our country great for everyone!"

So, Independence Day in the United States is not just about fireworks and parades. It is a birthday party for America. It is a thank you to the past. And it is a wish for a good future.

WHAT DID YOU LEARN?

Are these sentences **T**rue or **F**alse?

Independence Day is celebrated on July 4th.
On July 4th, America declared the war.
Before 1776, America was connected to Britain.
The American Revolution was a quick war.
The U.S. flag is red, white, and blue.
Families often have a special meal indoors.
Fireworks are a traditional part of this day.
On this day, people wear black clothes.
The leaders do not give any speeches on July 4th.
Independence Day is a big celebration for America.

PHRASAL VERB OF THE DAY

Get together: to meet and spend time with each other.

On Independence Day, families and friends get together for a special meal, usually outdoors.

YOUR NOTES:

_____

_____

_____

EXPLORING
DUBAI

"A CITY

OF WONDERS"

CHAPTER 9

EXPLORING DUBAI

Dubai is in a country called the United Arab Emirates, or UAE. Many people from different places live there. It was a small fishing place. People went fishing or looked for pearls in the sea. But then, something changed, when they found oil in the ground. Oil is very valuable, and it brought a lot of money to Dubai.

With money, Dubai started to grow. It wanted to become a special city. They built big buildings, roads, and parks. Now, Dubai is a place where the whole world wants to visit or live.

A famous building is the Burj Khalifa which is also the tallest building in the world. People can see everything from the top: the sea, the desert, and all of Dubai. It is a beautiful view, especially when the sun sets.

But, there is more! There is a place called the Dubai Mall. It is a huge shopping place. People buy clothes, eat food, and have fun. There is even an ice rink inside. And you can see a big water tank with fish. It looks like the ocean.

Close to this mall, water dances in the air in the Dubai Fountain Show. Water jumps high, music plays and lights change. It is a beautiful show that happens every night.

Do you know Dubai has islands that look like palm trees? One is the Palm Jumeirah. The houses there are big and beautiful. People also stay in nice hotels by the beach. The water is very blue and the sand is very white.

In Dubai, there is a famous hotel named Burj Al Arab. It looks like a sail on the sea. Inside, everything is rich and beautiful. People say it is more than a five-star hotel. It is like a dream.

Dubai does something interesting. It does not ask for many taxes. A tax is money people pay to the government. Because of this, many business people come to Dubai. They start companies and make more jobs. This plan works well. People have good jobs, and they make good money. They can buy things and enjoy life in Dubai. The city gets busier and richer every day.

But Dubai remembers history, too. There is an old place called Al Fahidi or "Bastakiya". The houses there are very old. People sell things they make by hand.

Dubai is like a magic city. It came from the sand and became a star. People work, build, and dream there. It shows us what can happen when we try to work hard.

WHAT DID YOU LEARN?

Are these sentences **T**rue or **F**alse?

In Dubai people went fishing.
Dubai changed after founding gold in the ground.
The Burj Khalifa is the tallest building in the world.
You can find an ice rink in the Dubai Mall.
The water in the Dubai Fountain dances in the air.
Palm Jumeirah is shaped like a circle.
The Burj Al Arab hotel looks like a sail on the sea.
People in Dubai do not pay any taxes at all.
Al Fahidi, is a modern part of Dubai.
Dubai is a city that came from the sand.

PHRASAL VERB OF THE DAY

Build up: start from little or nothing and gradually add more over time, until something becomes significant or impressive.

Dubai has built up its resources and infrastructure to become a globally recognised city.

YOUR NOTES:

_____

_____

_____

ALBERT
EINSTEIN

"GENIUS

AND

VISIONARY"

CHAPTER 10

ALBERT EINSTEIN

Albert Einstein was born on March 14, 1879 in a city called Ulm, in Germany. He was not just a famous scientist. He was one of the most important thinkers in history.

When Albert was a child, he was very curious. He always asked many questions even if he started talking when he was four and started reading when he was seven. His parents worried about him. But he was just thinking deeply.

At school, Albert was not the best student. Some subjects were boring for him. He loved math and science. He was very good at them. He went to school in Munich. Later, his family moved to Italy and he continued his studies in Switzerland.

In 1900, Albert finished his studies. He started to work in a patent office, a place where inventions are checked. He had a lot of time to think there. He wrote scientific papers in his free time.
1905 was a special year for Einstein. It was his "miracle year." He wrote four big science papers about new

ideas. These ideas changed science. One paper was about "special relativity". It talked about time, space, and speed. People started to notice Einstein after that.

Einstein became famous. He started to work at universities and moved to different countries. He taught students and wrote more science papers. He talked with other scientists. His ideas were very good.

In 1915, Einstein had another big idea. It was "general relativity". It was about gravity. Gravity is a force that pulls things down. This idea made Einstein more famous.

Einstein moved to the United States in 1933. He moved because Germany was a dangerous place at that time and a bad leader named Hitler was in charge. Einstein was Jewish and all the Jewish people were not safe in Germany. He went to work at a school called Princeton. It was in New Jersey.

In the United States, Einstein was famous and respected. He worked and taught at Princeton until 1945. World War II was happening and, even if he didn't like the war, he helped the United States. He wrote a letter to President Roosevelt talking about powerful weapons. This was important for the war.

Einstein got old. He died on April 18, 1955 in the United States. He was 76 years old. People all over the world were sad and remembered him. But his ideas stayed.

Today, we still use Einstein's ideas. They help us understand space. We know how stars and black holes work. We use his ideas in GPS too.

Einstein also helps us with energy. His famous idea, $E=mc^2$, says the matter can become energy. This idea is used in nuclear power. This power gives electricity. It is very strong.
Einstein's ideas also help doctors who use big machines to see inside our bodies. We also see Einstein's ideas in TVs and cameras too. TVs and cameras use a special light which was discovered by Einstein.

Many people respect Einstein today. Schools teach about him, books talk about him, movies show his life. People around the world know his name.

Einstein was not just a scientist. He wanted to make the world better. He gave us new ways to see the world and made big changes.

WHAT DID YOU LEARN?

Are these sentences **T**rue or **F**alse?

Albert Einstein was born on March 14, 1879, in Italy.
He didn't start speaking until he was four years old.
Einstein was the best student in all subjects at school.
He wrote four big science papers in 1905.
His paper on "special relativity" talked about time.
In 1915, Einstein wrote about gravity.
He moved to the US because it was dangerous.
He worked and taught in New York until 1945.
Einstein's ideas are not used today.
His famous equation $E=mc^2$ is about energy.

PHRASAL VERB OF THE DAY

Come up with: it is the process of creating, inventing, or thinking about new ideas.

Albert Einstein came up with some of the greatest ideas in the history of science, including the theory of relativity.

YOUR NOTES:

_____

_____

_____

CHRISTMAS AROUND THE WORLD

"A FESTIVE

JOY"

CHAPTER 11

CHRISTMAS AROUND THE WORLD

Christmas is a special time and people all around the world celebrate it. It is a holiday full of joy, lights, and happiness. Every country has its own way to celebrate. Here are how some countries enjoy Christmas.

The United States

In the United States, Christmas is very important. Families decorate their homes with lights. They put up huge Christmas trees. They hang socks, called "stockings," near the fireplace. Children believe that Santa Claus comes. He travels in a sleigh pulled by reindeer. He brings gifts and puts them under the tree. Families open the gifts on Christmas morning. They eat big meals with their families. They sing songs called "carols."

Australia

Christmas in Australia is different. December is summer there! It is very hot. People often go to the beach and they have barbecues. Australian children also believe in Santa Claus but sometimes they think he might wear a cooler outfit because of the heat. Australians hang wreaths on their doors. They also sing carols by candlelight. There are big outdoor concerts too.

Mexico
In Mexico, Christmas is colourful. It starts on December 12th and ends on January 6th. Families put up "nacimientos." These are scenes showing the birth of Jesus. Children play a game called "posada." They go from house to house. They sing to ask if Mary and Joseph can stay. People say no until the last house. There is a party there and they break a piñata. It is full of sweets.

Germany
Germans loves Christmas markets. There are lots of stalls in the streets full of lights. People buy decorations and gifts. They eat tasty food and drink a warm drink called "Glühwein", made of hot wine with spices. Families in Germany also celebrate the Advent. Children open a new door on the calendar each day and they get a small gift.

Philippines
The Philippines has the longest Christmas. It starts in September! They call their celebration "Pasko." People go to church very early for nine days. They eat a special rice cake called "bibingka." They hang out big lanterns called "parols" which are like stars in the night.

Sweden

In Sweden, there is a special day. It is on December 13th on St. Lucia's Day. Girls wear white dresses and a crown of lights. They bring coffee and pastries to families. In Sweden, families also have a big feast on Christmas Eve. They eat a lot of good food.

Italy

Christmas in Italy is about family and food. They have a big dinner on Christmas Eve. They do not eat meat but fish. Children wait for Santa Claus the 24th of December and a witch called "La Befana" in January. She flies on a broom and brings gifts. If children are bad, they get coal.

Brazil

In Brazil, they call Santa Claus "Papai Noel." Families go to midnight church services on Christmas. The weather is warm so many decorations have snowmen with sunglasses. People like to set off fireworks. They have big Christmas trees made of lights in the cities.

Japan

Christmas is not a holiday in Japan but people like to spread joy. They give presents and share a special cake. It is a sponge cake with cream and strawberries.

Every country has its own special way to celebrate Christmas. They have different food, traditions, and decorations but everyone is happy.

WHAT DID YOU LEARN?

Are these sentences **T**rue or **F**alse?

In the US, people decorate homes with lights.
Australians celebrate Christmas in the winter.
In Mexico, the celebration begins in December.
Germans celebrate by eating a special cold drink.
In the Philippines, the celebration is in September.
On St. Lucia's Day in Sweden, boys wear crowns.
In Italy, people have a big dinner with meat.
In Brazil, Santa Claus is known as "Papai Noel.
Christmas is an official holiday in Japan.
All countries celebrate Christmas in the same way.

PHRASAL VERB OF THE DAY

Put up: to place things in their positions.

Families decorate their homes with lights. They put up huge Christmas trees.

YOUR NOTES:

_____

_____

_____

COOBER PEDY

"THE LIFE

UNDERGROUND"

COOBER PEDY

Coober Pedy is a small town in Australia. It is very far from big cities and about 4,000 people live there. People know Coober Pedy because it is very hot. It is also known for special stones called opals.

Australia can be very hot but Coober Pedy is one of the hottest parts. The temperature can reach 50 Celsius degrees. The sun is very strong, and there is not much water. The weather can make life hard, but the people are strong.

Because it is so hot, people in Coober Pedy live underground. This means they make homes in the ground. These homes are cool and safe. They are like normal houses, but inside the earth. People have everything they need in them. They have rooms like kitchens, bedrooms, and living rooms.

A long time ago, people went to Coober Pedy to look for opals. There are a lot of them in the town. They are beautiful stones with many colors. People use them in jewelry. Finding opals is hard work. Sometimes, they find many opals together. They call this an "opal pocket." Workers use big machines to move the earth. Then they sell these stones for money. Tourists also come to buy opals.

Coober Pedy is far from hospitals but there are doctors who fly in airplanes. The service is called the "Royal Flying Doctor Service." When someone is sick or hurt, people call this service and they come quickly by plane. They have medicine and equipment in their planes. Sometimes, they take sick people to big hospitals. They work every day to keep people safe. This service is very important for everyone in Coober Pedy and remote parts of Australia.

There are big farms around Coober Pedy. People call these "stations". They are not like train stations but they are places where people keep animals. The most common animal is cattle. Cattle are big animals that people use for meat and milk.

Life on a station is busy. People take care of the cattle every day. They give them food and water. They make sure they are healthy.

Coober Pedy is not a busy town. There are not many people and it is quiet but it is not boring. People have sports like golf. But they play at night because of the heat. They use glowing balls to see them in the dark. They also have small stores for shopping. There are also places to eat out like cafes and restaurants. There are churches. But remember, everything is underground!

Many tourists come to see Coober Pedy. They want to see the underground homes and learn about opals. Some tourists try to find opals too. It is fun but not easy. Visitors can buy opals to take home.

Coober Pedy is different from other towns. It has heat, opals, and underground homes. People here are proud of their town. They are a strong community. They work hard, and they care for each other. Coober Pedy is a special place in the heart of Australia.

WHAT DID YOU LEARN?

Are these sentences **T**rue or **F**alse?

Coober Pedy is known for its cold weather.
People in Coober Pedy live overground.
Opals are stones that can be found nearby.
The Royal Flying Doctor Service helps animals.
There are big farms called "stations".
People play golf during the day in the heat.
Tourists come learn about opals.
Cattle are small animals farms.
There are no places to eat in Coober Pedy.
All the buildings in Coober Pedy are homes.

PHRASAL VERB OF THE DAY

Dig out: remove something from a buried place.

In Coober Pedy, people dig out homes from the earth to escape the extreme heat.

YOUR NOTES:

_____

_____

_____

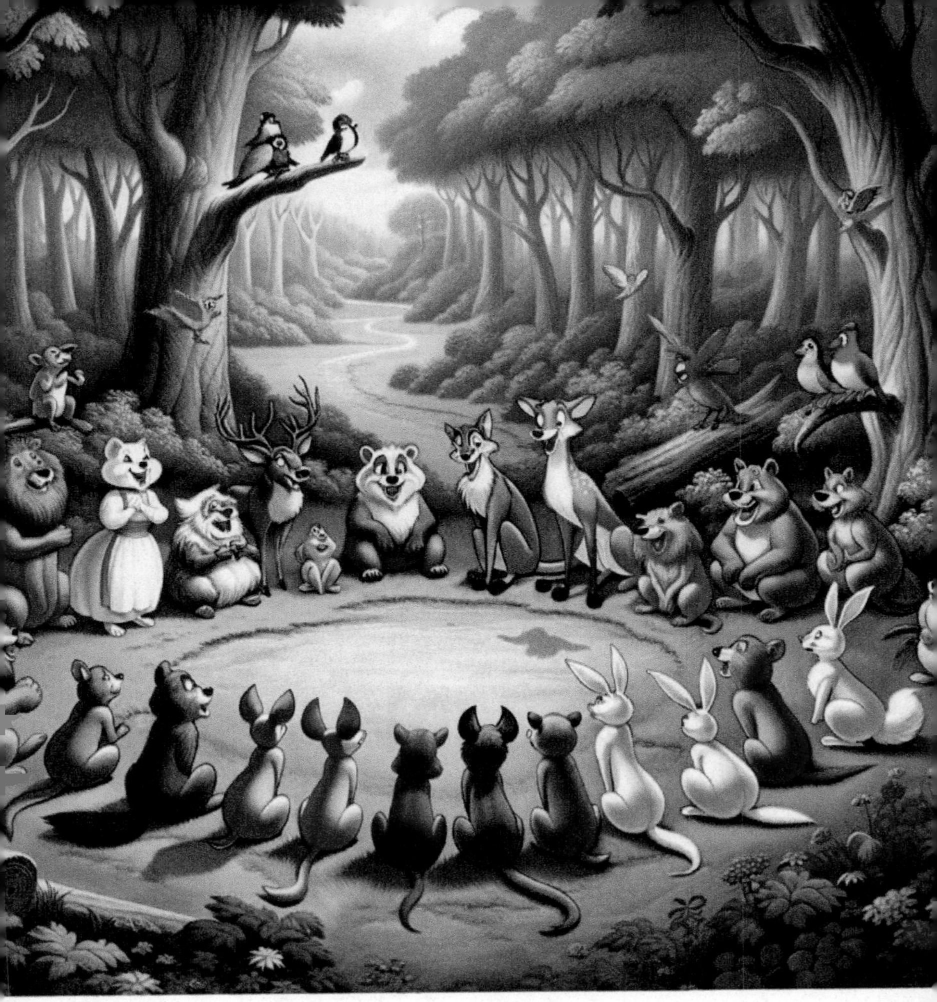

WALT DISNEY

"FAMILIES MUST HAVE FUN"

CHAPTER 13

WALT DISNEY

Walt Disney was a very famous man from America. He was born on December 5, 1901. He had a big dream to make people happy. He loved to draw and tell stories. This love made him create many cartoons. Some of these cartoons are still loved by many people today.

One of his first famous cartoons was Mickey Mouse. Mickey is a small, happy mouse with big ears. He has a dog named Pluto and many friends. One of his best friends is Minnie Mouse. They have many fun adventures together. People loved Mickey Mouse so much. They wanted to see more of him.

After Mickey Mouse, Walt Disney made many other cartoons. Some of these cartoons are Donald Duck, Goofy, and Snow White. Snow White was a special cartoon. It was the first full-length cartoon movie. People had never seen anything like it before.

Walt Disney also made comix. Comix are like books but with many pictures. In these comix, he told stories about his characters. People could read these comix and see the adventures of their favourite characters. In the comix, there are two interesting characters. Their names are Rockerduck and Paperon de'

Paperoni. Some people say that Rockerduck is like a real-life person named John D. Rockefeller. He was a very rich man in America. Paperon de' Paperoni is like another real-life person named Andrew Carnegie. He was also very rich. These two characters are very important in the comix.

Walt Disney had another big dream. He wanted to make a place where families could have fun. This place was called Disneyland. Disneyland is like a big playground with many rides. It also has places where people can see the characters from the cartoons. The first Disneyland opened in California in 1955. People loved it. It was like stepping into a cartoon world.

Today, there are many Disneyland parks around the world. People from all over come to visit. They want to see Mickey Mouse, ride the rides, and have fun. These parks are a big part of Walt Disney's dream.

Walt Disney passed away on December 15, 1966. But his dream lives on. His cartoons, comix, and Disneyland parks are still loved today. People remember him as a man who wanted to make the world a happier place. He used his talent to tell stories that make people smile and get together in his parks.

WHAT DID YOU LEARN?

Are these sentences **T**rue or **F**alse?

Walt Disney was born on December 5, 1901.
Walt Disney's first cartoon was Donald Duck.
Mickey Mouse is a happy mouse with big ears.
Snow White was the first full-length cartoon movie.
Walt Disney did not create any comix.
Rockerduck and P. de' Paperoni are in the comix.
Disneyland is a small playground with a few rides.
The first Disneyland opened in California in 1950.
There is only one Disneyland in the whole world.
Walt Disney is still alive today.

PHRASAL VERB OF THE DAY

Dream up: describe the process of coming up with an idea or invention in your imagination.

*Walt Disney **dreamed up** many beloved characters and stories, such as Mickey Mouse.*

YOUR NOTES:

_____

_____

_____

BITCOIN

"IS IT THE FUTURE OF MONEY?"

BITCOIN

Bitcoin is a kind of money but it is not like the money we use every day. It is called "digital money" or "cryptocurrency". This means it exists only on computers. It was created in 2009 by someone using the name Satoshi Nakamoto. No one really knows who this person is. It's a big mystery!

Bitcoin was made to be a new kind of money. It is not controlled by any government or bank. This is very different from the money we know. People liked the idea of having a kind of money that was free from control.

How do people get Bitcoin? They can buy it with regular money. They can also sell things and get paid in Bitcoin. Another way to get Bitcoin is by "mining". Mining is like a big computer puzzle. People use powerful computers to solve this puzzle. When they solve it, they get new Bitcoin. This is how new Bitcoin is made. It is like finding gold, but on a computer.

People keep their Bitcoin in a digital wallet. This wallet is on their computer or phone. They can send Bitcoin to other people or receive it. It is like sending an email, but with money.

There are good things about Bitcoin. One good thing is that it is fast. If you want to send money to someone far away, Bitcoin can do it quickly. Another good thing is privacy. With Bitcoin, people can keep their transactions private.

But, there are also not-so-good things about Bitcoin. One problem is that its value can change a lot. One day, one Bitcoin might be worth a lot of money. The next day, it might be worth less. This can be risky. Another problem is that some people use Bitcoin for bad things. They might buy or sell illegal things with it.

Bitcoin is produced all over the world. People who mine Bitcoin are in many countries. They use big computer centers to mine. These computer centers need a lot of electricity and this is why mining takes a lot of power. Some people worry about the use of too much electricity.

What about the future of Bitcoin? Many people have different ideas. Some people think it will be used more and more. They think many people will start using Bitcoin instead of regular money. Other people are not so sure. They think Bitcoin might have problems in the future.

There are also other digital moneys like Bitcoin. They are called "altcoins". Some of these are Ethereum, Ripple, and Litecoin. These are like Bitcoin's little brothers and sisters. They work in similar ways but have some differences.

Bitcoin is a new kind of money. It has changed the way some people think about money. It has good points and not-so-good points. The future of Bitcoin is still a question. But one thing is sure: it has made many people think differently about money and how it works.

WHAT DID YOU LEARN?

Are these sentences **T**rue or **F**alse?

Bitcoin is the same as everyday's money.
Bitcoin exists only on computers.
We know who created Bitcoin.
Any government controls Bitcoin.
People can buy Bitcoin with regular money.
You can keep Bitcoin in a digital wallet.
The value of Bitcoin never changes.
Mining Bitcoin uses a lot of electricity.
Bitcoin is the only kind of digital money.
All people agree about the future of Bitcoin.

PHRASAL VERB OF THE DAY

Carry out: to complete a task or execute an action.

People carry out transactions using Bitcoin by sending and receiving it in their digital wallets.

YOUR NOTES:

_____

_____

_____

THE WORLD
OF FASHION

"EXPRESSIVE

BUT

EXPENSIVE"

THE WORLD OF FASHION

People all over the world love fashion. Fashion means making, selling, and buying clothes. Some clothes are simple, some are fancy. Fashion is different in every country and many people follow big fashion brands. These brands tell people what is trendy. Trendy means very popular and stylish.

Some top fashion brands are known everywhere. These brands include Chanel, Louis Vuitton, and Gucci. They make very beautiful clothes and bags. Many people dream about buying their products. These brands show their new clothes at fashion shows and they decide what the next fashion will be.

Fashion shows are very big events. They happen in different cities. The three cities that are very famous for fashion shows are Paris, Milan, and New York. These are called the "Big Three" of fashion. Many people go the fashion shows and see the new clothes.

Paris is a city in France where the biggest fashion brands have shows. It is important for fashion history.

Many famous fashion ideas started in Paris. People who love fashion must visit Paris.

Milan is a city in Italy very important for fashion. Italian fashion is about luxury which means very expensive and nice. In Milan, brands show beautiful, expensive clothes. Italian style is known for looking rich and bold. People see many colors and designs in Milan. The city is full of fashion all the time.

The fashion in New York is new and exciting. People see many different styles in New York. This city likes new fashion ideas. It is a good place for young fashion designers.

Italy has a big role in the fashion world. It has many famous fashion schools. People come to Italy to learn about fashion. Italy teaches them about quality that means how good something is. Italian clothes and bags use very good materials. They look good, and they last a long time. Italy has a history of making beautiful things.

Some people in fashion are very rich. They have a lot of money because they sell many clothes and bags. Bernard Arnault is one of these people. He is in charge of a big fashion company. Amancio Ortega is another rich person in fashion. He sells different kinds of clothes around the world. These people show that fashion can make a lot of money.

Today, fashion is changing. The internet is very important and a lot of people buy clothes online. So fashion brands use Instagram and other apps to promote their clothes online. People see these clothes and want to buy them.

Fashion bloggers are new fashion stars. They are not famous like movie stars but they have many followers on the internet. They show clothes and tell people what they look like. They can influence people to buy those clothes.

Fashion is important for culture. It is more than just clothes. It is about ideas and expressing ourselves. The feeling of wearing something beautiful never changes.

WHAT DID YOU LEARN?

Are these sentences **T**rue or **F**alse?

Fashion is only about making clothes.
Only one country has fashion brands.
Chanel is a well-known fashion brand.
Fashion shows happen only in Paris.
Paris and New York are famous for their shows.
Italian style is known for being luxurious.
All fashion designers are from New York.
People can learn about fashion in Italy.
Bernard Arnault has a small fashion business.
Fashion bloggers are very popular on the internet.

PHRASAL VERB OF THE DAY

Dress up: to wear special clothes, especially to look more formal, attractive, or stylish than usual.

For fashion shows in cities like Paris or Milan, people often dress up in their most stylish outfits.

YOUR NOTES:

_____

_____

_____

THE MEDIEVAL LIFE

"A HOPEFUL LIFE"

THE MEDIEVAL LIFE

The medieval period, also known as the Middle Ages, lasted from the 5th to the late 15th century. Life back then was very different from today, and many things happened during this time. People lived in different places like castles, villages, and farms. There were also famous events, changes in how people ate and dressed, and the big city of Rome was very important.

Life in the castles

Castles were big houses where the king or lord and his family lived. They were like small villages. Inside the walls, there were gardens, animals, and people working. These people helped run the castle. They were soldiers, cooks, and cleaners. The walls around the castle were high to keep enemies out. The life in castles was safe, but it was also hard. People had to work a lot.

Kids in castles learned how to be good knights or ladies. Boys practiced fighting and riding horses. Girls learned how to manage a house and make beautiful crafts. They did not go to school like us. Teachers came to the castle.

Famous events

One big event was the "Black Death." It was a very bad sickness that came to Europe in the 14th century. Many people got sick and died. It changed how people lived because there were not many workers left.

Another important time was called the "Crusades." This was when soldiers from Europe fought to win lands far away. They went on long trips to fight for many years that changed the way countries worked together.

The role of Rome

Rome was a powerful city. In the Middle Ages, Rome was important for the church. The church was a big part of everyone's life and its leader lived in Rome. He was called the Pope. The Pope was very strong and even kings listened to him.

People went on trips to Rome which were called "pilgrimages." They went to pray and see the church buildings. They believed this helped them be safe and happy.

Eating and dressing

People ate different food in the Middle Ages. They did not have refrigerators, so they ate what they could find or grow. Rich people in castles ate meat, bread, and sweet things. Poor people ate soup, vegetables, and a little meat. At a big meal in a castle, many people sat together. They did not have plates like us. They used bread to hold their food.

They also did not use forks. They ate with their hands or knives.

How people dressed showed if they were rich or poor. Rich people had clothes from nice cloth like silk. They wore many colours. Poor people wore clothes from a plant called "wool." Their clothes were simple.

Famous people

In the Middle Ages, there were famous people, too. One was a man named "William the Conqueror", the King in England who fought a big battle to be king. Another person was "Joan of Arc." She was a young girl, but she helped soldiers in France. She wore armor and helped during a big war with England. People remember her because she was brave.

"Marco Polo" was also famous. He did not fight but he travelled. Marco went on long trips to far places. He even went to China! When he came back, he told stories about what he saw.

The Middle Ages were a busy time. People built big, beautiful buildings that we can still see today. They fought wars, worked hard, and made art. Today, we can remember these famous people and learn about life in the castles.

WHAT DID YOU LEARN?

Are these sentences **T**rue or **F**alse?

Castles were small homes where the king lived.
Boys learned to fight and girls learned household.
The "Black Death" made many deaths.
The "Crusades" were peaceful wars.
The Pope was a powerful person in Rome.
People used refrigerators to keep food fresh.
Rich people wore clothes made from silk.
"William the Conqueror" was a King in England.
"Joan of Arc" was a traveller who got to China.
People built big buildings that still stand today.

PHRASAL VERB OF THE DAY

Set out: to indicate the beginning of a trip or departure.

Pilgrims set out for Rome to see the church buildings and pray.

YOUR NOTES:

_____

_____

_____

THE ROMAN
EMPIRE

"LEADERS

OF THE WORLD"

THE ROMAN EMPIRE

The Roman Empire was a powerful time in history. It started a long time ago, around 27 BC, and lasted for many centuries.

Rome was a very important place. Lots of people lived there, rich and poor. The streets were full of people, animals, and carts. There were big buildings called temples and places for shopping called markets. Rich people had big houses with beautiful rooms. They had paintings and comfortable furniture. Poor people lived in small houses with just one or two rooms. They were very crowded.

In Rome, there were special games and fights for fun. These took place in a big building called the Colosseum. People went there to watch and cheer. It was like a big party.

Life in other towns

There were many towns in the Roman Empire where the life was different. The houses were not so big, and the streets were quiet. People in towns knew each other. They worked together and helped each other. In these towns, people had jobs like farming, making things, or selling things. The towns had walls around them for safety. At night, the gates were locked. This kept the people safe from danger.

Eating in the Roman Empire
Food was important for everyone. Rich people had big dinners with many things. They ate meat, fish, vegetables, and sweet desserts. They had cooks who made their food. They ate lying down on sofas and talked with friends.

Poor people did not have big dinners. They ate simple food like bread, cheese, and vegetables. Sometimes, they had fish or chicken. They cooked at home in small kitchens. Families ate together, sitting around the table.

Dressing up and acting
Rich men wore a long piece of cloth called a toga. Women wore long dresses called stolas. These clothes were made from nice material and had colours.

Poor people wore simple clothes. They had tunics, which were like long shirts. They were not colourful because dye was expensive.

How people acted was important, too. When men met, they shook hands. Friends hugged. In public, people had to be polite and quiet when someone important was speaking. Children were to be seen and not heard when adults were talking.

Rich and poor people
In the Roman Empire, some people were very rich. They had lots of money and many slaves to work for them. The slaves did everything - cooking, cleaning, and more. Rich people did not work. They had

parties, went to shows, and enjoyed baths in big bathhouses.

Poor people had to work hard. They were farmers, builders, or servants. They did not have slaves. Life was hard for them, but they had small joys. They loved their families and enjoyed festivals in the town.

Famous people in Roman times
"Julius Caesar" was a strong leader. He fought in many battles and won. He became the ruler of Rome. People knew him because he was smart and brave.
"Augustus" was the first Emperor of Rome. He was Julius Caesar's adopted son. He made Rome peaceful and rich. He built many roads and buildings.
"Cleopatra" was a queen but not in Rome. She was in Egypt. She was smart and spoke many languages. She met Julius Caesar and they became friends.

"Nerone" was an emperor, too. But he is famous because he was not a good man. He did bad things, like hurting people. Some say he started a big fire in Rome.

The Roman Empire was a big part of history. Life then was full of interesting things. Some people in Rome were famous because they did great things. Some were famous for not being good. But together, they have made the story of the Roman Empire very exciting. We still remember them and talk about their lives.

WHAT DID YOU LEARN?

Are these sentences **T**rue or **F**alse?

The Roman Empire began around 27 BC.
In Rome, nobody lived in small houses.
The Colosseum was used for fun events.
All towns were loud and crowded.
Rich people had big dinners with much food.
Poor people usually wore colourful clothes.
Julius Caesar was a famous leader at that time.
Cleopatra was the queen of Rome.
All people in the Roman Empire were rich.
The Roman Empire was an important part of history.

PHRASAL VERB OF THE DAY

Fight off: to defend against an attack by fighting against the attackers.

Julius Caesar had to fight off many enemies to keep Rome safe.

YOUR NOTES:

_____

_____

_____

BIODIVERSITY
IN AUSTRALIA

"SOME UNIQUE ANIMALS"

BIODIVERSITY IN AUSTRALIA

Australia is a big country with many different animals. It has a lot of biodiversity. Biodiversity means many types of living things. In Australia, you can find animals that live nowhere else.

People live and work in big cities but you don't see many strange animals. Out the cities, Australia is very different. There are places called "stations." These are like big farms. People at stations work with animals like cows and sheep.

So there are many more animals and some are very strange. One is the kangaroo. Kangaroos have big legs and can jump very far. They live in groups. Baby kangaroos live in their mother's pouch. People from other countries love to see kangaroos.

Another strange animal is the koala. Koalas are not bears, but they look a little like them. They have grey fur and big noses. Koalas live in trees. They sleep during the day. At night, they eat leaves. The leaves are from the eucalyptus tree. These trees smell very nice.

Australia also has many colorful birds. One bird is the kookaburra. It has a loud laugh. People can hear kookaburras in the morning. Another bird is the cockatoo. Cockatoos are white and very loud. They can also talk! They repeat words they hear from people.

But not all animals in Australia are friendly. Some are dangerous. One dangerous animal is the snake. There are many snakes in Australia. Some snakes have poison. If they bite, it is a big problem and you need to go to the hospital very fast.

When people find dangerous animals like snakes or spiders, they must be careful. They should not touch or chase the animals. It is important to stay calm. They can call animal experts who know how to catch the animals safely.

In the sea, there are also many animals. Some are big like whales. People can see whales when they swim by the coast. It is very exciting to watch. There are also dolphins. Dolphins are friendly and smart. They sometimes play with people in the water.

But the sea also has dangerous animals. One is the shark. Sharks are big and strong. People should be careful when they swim in the sea. If there is a shark, they need to get out of the water. The beach might close for a while. People can go back in when it is safe.

Another sea animal is the jellyfish. Some jellyfish have poison. It can hurt to touch them. If a jellyfish stings someone, they need help. Vinegar can help with the sting. It is good to know what to do.

Australia cares about its animals. There are laws to protect them. It is not fine to hurt the animals. There are also parks just for wildlife. These are big areas where animals can live safely. People can go to watch the animals. It is important not to leave trash in these parks.

Schools in Australia teach kids about animals. Kids learn their names and which animals are dangerous. They also learn how to be safe. It is good for kids to know about nature.

Australia is full of amazing animals, some are cute and some are dangerous. But all are important for the life of the planet. Everyone in the world loves Australia's biodiversity.

WHAT DID YOU LEARN?

Are these sentences **T**rue or **F**alse?

Australia is known for its low level of biodiversity.
Kangaroos are unique to Australia.
Koalas are a species of bear that live in Australia.
Kookaburras are recognised for their loud laugh.
All snakes in Australia are non-venomous.
It's recommended to chase dangerous animals.
In Australia, you can see whales from the coast.
All sharks are considered harmless to humans.
In case of a jellyfish sting, using vinegar can help.
There are no legal protections for wildlife.

PHRASAL VERB OF THE DAY

Ward off: to prevent something from harming you or keep it at a distance.

Hikers in Australia carry snake repellent to ward off any potential bites while trekking through the wilderness.

YOUR NOTES:

_____

_____

_____

THE ENGLISH
CAB

"A NARRATIVE

JOURNEY "

THE ENGLISH CAB

The story of the English cab is very interesting. A long time ago, the first cabs were not cars. They were horse-drawn carriages. These were called "hackney carriages." People did not call a phone to get a cab. They went into the street and when they saw a carriage, they waved. The carriage stopped and they got in. The driver, called a "cabbie," knew many streets. The cabbie took people where they wanted to go. The carriage was for everyone, not just rich people. It was like a bus today.

In the old days, there were rules for cabbies. The rules said how much money the ride was. There was a rule for the horses, too. Horses could not work too many hours. This was because people loved animals and did not want them to be tired.

Years went by, and there were new ideas. People wanted faster and better cabs so the first cars came to the streets. They were not fast like cars today. They made much noise and smoke. But it was a beginning.

The new cabs had a meter that showed how much money the ride was. It was fair. The cabbie turned on the meter, and it started to count the money so the person in the cab could see it.

There were more rules now. They had to know all the streets. They had to know where places were, like hotels, stations, and schools. The test for this was hard. People called it "The Knowledge." Cabbies studied for many years for it.

The English cab today is very modern. The cabs now are safe and clean. They are good for the environment. Some cabs use electricity. They do not use gas. This is because people understand that clean air is important.

Cabs today have new colours. The old cabs were mostly black. Now, cabs are yellow, green, and more. They have ads on them. The ads are pictures that talk about other things you can buy or do.

Inside the cab, there are more changes. Now, there is a screen. The screen talks to the cabbie. It tells them where to go. Before, cabbies used a big map. Now, the map is on the screen. It is easier this way.

People do not only wave for cabs now. They use a phone or an app. The app tells them where the cab is so they know when the cab will come. It is very smart.

Cabbies are still important. They are friendly. They help people with bags. They find the fastest way to go. Sometimes, they talk about the weather or the news. People like this. It makes the ride nice.

What will happen next? Nobody knows. But people have dreams. Maybe cabs will drive themselves. Maybe they will fly. Maybe they will not make any noise at all.

The English cab is not just a ride. It is a part of the city's heart. It saw wars, parties, sad times, and happy times. It helped many people. It will continue to help many more. It is a symbol of movement, help, and progress.

WHAT DID YOU LEARN?

Are these sentences **T**rue or **F**alse?

The first cabs had horses.
People used a phone to find a cab.
Old cabs were only for rich people.
Horses could work all day and night without rest.
The first car cabs were very fast.
Today's cabs can use electricity.
All English cabs are black now.
Cabbies needed a big paper map before.
People can use an app to get a cab today.
Maybe in the future, cabs will fly.

PHRASAL VERB OF THE DAY

Pick up: to come to get a passenger and then drive them to their destination.

When someone needs a cab, the cabbie stops to pick them up and then takes them where they want to go.

YOUR NOTES:

_____

_____

_____

THE KNIGHTS OF THE ROUND TABLE

"WE ARE ALL

THE SAME"

THE KNIGHTS OF THE ROUND TABLE

In a land called England, there is an old, magical story about brave knights and a special table. They were called the "Knights of the Round Table." Their leader was King Arthur. Together, they went on amazing adventures.

King Arthur was a good king. He wanted peace and happiness for his people. He lived in a big castle called Camelot. In this castle, there was a special room with a big and round table. A round table has no head. Everyone is equal. King Arthur wanted all his knights to be equal. That's why he had a round table.

The Knights of the Round Table were special. They were brave and strong. They wore metal clothes called armour and carried big swords. They had a strict code of rules to respect.
It said: "Protect the weak, be honest, be brave and respect all people".

The knights followed this code. They helped people. They fought against bad people. They were heroes. One of the most famous knight was Sir Lancelot. He was one of the best knights. He was brave and strong. He won many fights. But he also loved King Arthur's queen, Guinevere. This love made problems.

There was a special person in King Arthur's life. His name was Merlin. He was not a knight. He was a wizard. A wizard is a person with magic powers. Merlin helped King Arthur. He gave him advice. He told him about the future. He also gave him a special sword. This sword was called "Excalibur." It was a strong and magical sword. With this sword, King Arthur won many battles.

The Knights of the Round Table had many adventures. They went to far places. They met dragons, giants, and other magical creatures. They saved people. They found treasures. But they also had challenges. Challenges are like big problems. Sometimes, the knights had to fight. Sometimes, they had to think. But they always helped each other. They were like brothers.

Every story has an end. The story of King Arthur and his knights is sad. There were fights between the knights caused by problems with love. There were also enemies outside the castle. In the end, King Arthur had a big battle against another knight named Mordred. King Arthur won, but he was hurt. He went to a magical place called Avalon. Some say he slept there. Some say he will come back one day.

The Knights of the Round Table are not just a story. They teach us about friendship and bravery. They show us that it is important to be good. It is important to help others.

WHAT DID YOU LEARN?

Are these sentences **T**rue or **F**alse?

The "Knights of the Round Table" lived in England.
King Arthur lived in a house in the countryside.
The round table meant that everyone was equal.
The code included being honest and kind.
Sir Lancelot disliked Queen Guinevere.
Merlin helped King Arthur in battles.
King Arthur's special sword was named "Excalibur."
The knights never had to face any challenges.
King Arthur was defeated in a battle by Mordred.
The story teaches about courage and friendship.

PHRASAL VERB OF THE DAY

Take on: ready to start a challenge or battle with someone or something.

In the end, King Arthur had a big battle and took on another knight named Mordred.

YOUR NOTES:

_____

_____

_____

MOUNT
EVEREST

"GODDESS

MOTHER

OF THE WORLD"

MOUNT EVEREST

Mount Everest is the highest mountain in the world. It is so tall, it reaches above the clouds. It is in a place called the Himalayas, between two countries, Nepal and China. Many climbers from around the world dream about going to the top. The journey is hard and dangerous, but also exciting.

Climbers need strong bodies and minds. The journey on Mount Everest is cold and long. They wear big coats, gloves, and special boots. They carry heavy bags on their backs. Inside the bags are food, water, and things to help them climb.

Climbers train for many months. They learn to breathe when the air is thin. There is not much air high on the mountain. They eat lots of food to be strong. They practice climbing and walking with heavy bags.

It takes many days to climb Mount Everest so people need places to sleep, called camps. There are four main camps on Mount Everest. They are named Camp 1, Camp 2, Camp 3, and Camp 4. Each camp is higher up the mountain.

The camps have tents which are small and simple. They protect from the wind and snow. Inside the tents, climbers have sleeping bags. These sleeping bags are very warm.

Climbers rest at camps. They eat, sleep, and talk to their friends. They also check their health. It is important to feel good before climbing more.

Sherpas are very important on Mount Everest. They are people who live in Nepal, near the mountain. They know the mountain very well, they know how to stay safe, so help climbers. They carry heavy bags and show the way. They are strong and brave.

Sherpas also set up the tents at the camps. They cook food for the climbers. They encourage them when the journey is hard.

Sherpas have a deep respect for Mount Everest. They call it "Chomolungma." It means "Goddess Mother of the World." Sherpas and climbers have a special ceremony before climbing. They ask the mountain for safe passage. It is part of their tradition.

In the year 2015 there was a big earthquake in Nepal. It was strong and reached Mount Everest. It caused an avalanche that hit the base camp. Many people were buried and some died.

Mount Everest is amazing. Climbers still dream about reaching the top. Mount Everest teaches them about nature, life, and themselves. It is more than a mountain. It is a journey of the heart and spirit.

WHAT DID YOU LEARN?
Are these sentences **T**rue or **F**alse?

Mount Everest is the tallest mountain in the world.
Mount Everest is located in the United States.
People who climb need weak bodies.
There are two main camps on Mount Everest.
Sherpas are local people who help climbers.
The climbers carry light bags.
"Chomolungma" means "Goddess Mother."
There was a small earthquake in Nepal in 2015.
Sherpas do not respect Mount Everest.
People have a special ceremony before climbing.

PHRASAL VERB OF THE DAY

Climb up: to go up a mountain, a ladder, stairs, or any form of high structure.

Every year, hundreds of adventurers climb up Mount Everest, facing hard conditions and extreme challenges.

YOUR NOTES:

_____

_____

_____

OLD LIFE IN ENGLAND

"THE KING CARED OF PEOPLE"

OLD LIFE IN ENGLAND

Old England and London have many stories to tell. This place was special and full of life. Rich people lived differently from poor people. The king was important too. He was a father to the land. He took care of everyone. And there were interesting behaviors and traditions.

Old England and London

Old England was full of beautiful green lands, castles, and villages. London was the biggest city. It had a river called the Thames. Boats sailed on this river. The streets were busy. People walked, talked, and sold things in markets.

Life of rich people

Rich people in Old England had big houses or castles. Their homes had many rooms. Some rooms were for eating, some for sleeping. The walls had colourful paintings. The floors had soft carpets.

They wore beautiful clothes. Men wore coats and hats. Women wore long dresses with jewels. They had parties with music and dancing. They invited their friends to these parties. They ate tasty foods like meat, fruits, and desserts.

Rich people had horses to travel. Some even had carriages. A carriage is like a big box with wheels. Horses pull it. They also had servants. Servants helped in cooking, cleaning, and more.

Life of poor people
Poor people in Old England lived differently. Their houses were small. Sometimes, many families lived in one house. They had few rooms. Their clothes were simple. They did not have jewels or soft carpets.

Poor people worked hard. Some were farmers. They grew food for everyone. They made things like shoes, clothes, or pots. In London, some sold things in markets. They woke up early and went to bed late.

They ate simple foods. Bread, vegetables, and sometimes fish. They did not have big parties. But they loved their families and friends. They sang songs and told stories.

The role of the King
The king was very important in Old England. He lived in a big palace in London. It was beautiful
with big gardens. The king made big decisions for the country. People listened to him.
The king had helpers called knights. Knights wore metal clothes called armour and they had big horses. They protected the king and the land. Sometimes,

the king gave them special lands. They became lords of these lands.

Behaviours and traditions

People in Old England had behaviours and traditions. When they met, they said, "Good day." They were polite. Men took off their hats when they met women. Women curtsied. A curtsy is when a woman bends her knees a little.

Festivals were special. There was a festival called "May Day." People danced around a big pole with ribbons. It was fun. There was another one in winter. It was called "Christmas." People gave gifts, sang songs, and ate special food.

In London, there was a big clock called "Big Ben." It told time with loud bells. People looked at it to know the time. Another tradition was afternoon tea. At a certain time in the afternoon, people drank tea. They ate small cakes with it. It was a time to relax and chat.

People were proud of their home. They loved their green lands and busy streets. They respected their king and followed traditions. Life was simple, but it was full of love and happiness.

WHAT DID YOU LEARN?

Are these sentences **T**rue or **F**alse?

Rich people and poor people lived the same way.
The Thames is a big river in London.
Rich had helpers for cooking and cleaning.
Poor people in Old England lived in big houses.
The king had a small house with no gardens.
Knights helped keep the king safe.
Men took off their hats for women in Old England.
People danced with ribbons on "May Day".
People drank tea and ate cakes in the afternoon.
Big Ben was a big clock and told people the time.

PHRASAL VERB OF THE DAY

Show off: when someone displays something proudly or wants others to see what they have.

Rich people in Old England loved to show off their big houses, beautiful clothes, and expensive jewels to demonstrate their wealth and status.

YOUR NOTES:

_____

_____

THE TOP 5 DISCOVERIES

"HOW THE WORLD HAS CHANGED"

THE TOP 5 DISCOVERIES

The fire

Imagine a world without warm food. Imagine cold nights with no heat. This was the world before fire. People think that a long time ago, humans saw fire from lightning. They learned to use it. Fire was like magic. It gave warmth and light. It helped people cook food. This made the food taste better. It also made it safer to eat. Fire protected people from wild animals. People sat around the fire. They told stories. They became families and friends. Fire brought people together. It helped them live in cold places. It changed the way we live and eat. Fire is very important in our history.

The printing press machine

A long time ago, people wrote books by hand. This was very slow. It took many months to make just one book. Then, a man named Johannes Gutenberg had a new idea. He made the printing press machine. This machine was very special. It could make many books quickly. Now, more people could read and learn. Books became cheaper. Many people started to read. This changed everything. People learned about new places and ideas. The printing press machine made the world smarter.

The vaccine

Many years ago, there were bad diseases. People got sick easily. Many people died. It was very sad. Doctors wanted to help. They looked for ways to stop the diseases. Then, a man name Pasteur found a way. It was called a vaccine. A vaccine is like a shield. It protects people from diseases. When people get a vaccine, they do not get sick from that disease. The first vaccine was for a disease called smallpox. After this, more vaccines were made. Today, we have vaccines for many diseases. Children get vaccines when they are young. This helps them stay healthy. Vaccines have saved many lives. They changed the world. They made it safer.

Electricity

Think about your house. Think about the lights, the TV, and the fridge. All these need something. They need electricity. Before electricity, nights were dark. People used candles. Candles were not very bright. People went to sleep early. Then people found a way to use electricity. It was a big discovery. Thomas Edison made the light bulb that used electricity to give light. It changed everything. Now, homes were bright at night. People could read and work. Factories used electricity. Trains and trams used electricity. Today, everything uses electricity. Our phones, our cars, our computers. Electricity makes our world work. It changed how we live and work.

The internet

Today, we talk to people far away. We see pictures from other countries. We learn new things every day. All this is because of the internet. The internet is like a big library. But it is not just books. It is videos, music, and games. It is news and stories. The internet connects people. A person in England can talk to a person in India. They can be friends. They can learn from each other. Before the internet, this was not easy. The internet changed business, too. People buy things from other countries. They work with people from all over the world. Schools use the internet. Children learn new things. They see places they never saw before. The internet made the world closer. It made it easier to share and learn.

All these discoveries changed the world. They made life better. They helped people learn and grow. The world is always changing. Surely there will be new discoveries soon. We can only wait and see.

WHAT DID YOU LEARN?

Are these sentences **T**rue or **F**alse?

Before fire, people could not eat warm food.
Fire was discovered after seeing it from the sun.
The printing press machine made books rare.
Johannes Gutenberg invented the press machine.
Pasteur discovered the first vaccine for a disease.
Vaccines protect people from any kind of sickness.
People used candles to light places.
Thomas Edison discovered electricity.
The internet is only used for reading books.
The internet made it difficult to communicate.

PHRASAL VERB OF THE DAY

Come across: to find something or someone by chance.

Humans came across fire after seeing it from a lightning.

YOUR NOTES:

_____

_____

_____

THE NORTHERN LIGHTS

"A MAGIC FROM THE NATURE"

CHAPTER 24

 TRACK 24

THE NORTHERN LIGHTS

The Northern Lights are a beautiful show in the sky. They are also called "Aurora Borealis." They are like magic. And have many colours. They can be green, pink, purple, white, and red. They look like curtains moving in the wind. It is a combination of the Earth and the Sun talking.

The Northern Lights do not come out all the time. They like the dark night. People can see them in some cold countries far in the North like Norway, Iceland, Canada, and Finland. The best time to see the lights is in winter. This time is from September to March.

Many people want to see the Northern Lights so they travel to the North for a long journey. So, there are trips just to see the lights. People call this "Northern Lights tourism." It is very popular. It brings many people to the North.

People can choose different trips. Some are short, some are long. The trips have guides who know a lot about the lights. They know the best places to see them. They tell stories about the lights. They say what makes the lights. People learn a lot on these trips.

People do many things on these trips. They stay in special hotels made of ice. Some hotels have rooms in the snow like big tents. They are called "igloos." They are very quiet. At night, people can see the lights from their beds. It is very romantic.

People also ride in sleds with dogs in the inner forest. Then they look at the stars waiting for the lights. The sky is very big and full of stars. It is very beautiful.

Some people like to take photos. You need a special camera that can see in the dark and can take a picture of the lights. People have these pictures forever. They show their friends and family. They remember the trip.

To make this trip special, people eat food from the North,   sit by the fire and talk to local people. They learn about life in the cold. They also see wild animals, the snow and the mountains. They enjoy the quiet and the clean air. They forget their problems.

The Northern Lights make people feel small. They are a big and beautiful show. They are a mystery. They bring many people together who come from far away. They all will carry the dance in their hearts.

WHAT DID YOU LEARN?
Are these sentences **T**rue or **F**alse?

The Lights is the same as the Aurora Borealis.
The Northern Lights can only be seen in summer.
People travel to south to see the Lights.
Northern Lights tourism is very popular.
People can stay in big tents made of snow.
People cannot see the lights from their ice beds.
During the trip, people ride on horses.
Special cameras are needed to take pictures.
People do not interact with the local communities.
The Northern Lights make people feel very big.

PHRASAL VERB OF THE DAY

Light up: illuminate or make brighter.

The Northern Lights light up the night sky in beautiful colours.

YOUR NOTES:

_____

_____

_____

ATTILA

"A KING

WITHOUT

A CROWN"

ATTILA

Attila was a very famous leader a long time ago. He was not a king with a crown, but a powerful man. He was the leader of a group called the Huns. The Huns were strong fighters. They came from a place called the steppes of Central Asia. It was big open land.

Attila was born many years after Jesus Christ. Historians, think he was born after 400 years. They are not sure about the year and the place. He had a big family. His father's name is not known. His uncle was called Rua. Rua was a leader too. Attila had a brother, Bleda. They were close but also different. Attila was smart and strong. People do not know about his mother. It is a mystery.

Attila and Bleda became leaders when their uncle died. They made decisions to protect their people. The Huns looked up to them. Attila was more famous than Bleda so people talked about him more.

Attila did not live in a castle. He had strong horses. He liked to fight and to win. He was a real warrior. He wanted more power and more land. This made him rich.

The leader of the Romans was Theodosius. He was scared so made a deal with Attila. He gave Attila gold in change of peace.

So Attila did not stay quiet and went to a place called Gaul. Gaul is the old name of France. People in Gaul fought Attila and had a big battle. It was called the Battle of Catalaunian Plains. It was hard for Attila.

After Gaul, Attila looked at Italy. Italy was beautiful with good land. It had rich cities. Attila went there with his soldiers. They fought. They won some fights but lost others. People in Italy were very scared of the Huns.

As he was getting old, Attila started to think about life, about death. One day, something sad happened. Attila died. People do not know how he died. Some say he was sick. Some say he was killed. It is a mystery from history. When Attila died, things changed.

People will never forget Attila. Some say he was a bad king, some no. Books talk about him. Movies show his life. He is like a legend.
Attila's life was like a storm. It was fast. It was loud. It changed things. The world was not the same. Attila showed what one man can do.

WHAT DID YOU LEARN?

Are these sentences True or False?

Attila was a leader of a group called the Huns.
He had a small family with only one brother.
He became a leader after his father.
Attila and his people lived in big castles.
Attila wanted to have more land and power.
The leader of the Romans gave Attila a lot of gold.
Attila did not fight with the people in Gaul.
Attila died as a very old man.
Attila had a lot of children.
People still talk about Attila today.

PHRASAL VERB OF THE DAY

Take over: to assume control or responsibility for something, like a territory or a leadership position.

When his uncle died, Attila took over as the leader of the Huns, starting a new period of conquests and battles across Europe.

YOUR NOTES:

_____

_____

_____